TIKA
THE IGGY

LAURENCE KING

First published in Great Britain in 2023
by Laurence King, an imprint of
The Orion Publishing Group Ltd
Carmelite House, 50 Victoria
Embankment, London EC4Y 0DZ

An Hachette UK Company

10 9 8 7 6 5 4 3 2 1

A CIP catalogue record for this book
is available from the British Library.

ISBN 978-1-3996-0692-9

Senior Editor: Katherine Pitt
Design: Hannah Owens

Origination by F1 Colour Ltd, UK
Printed in China by C&C Offset Printing Co. Ltd.

www.laurenceking.com
www.orionbooks.co.uk

TIKA
THE IGGY

LESSONS IN LIFE, LOVE, AND FASHION

Laurence King Publishing

Contents

INTRO-
DUCTION

Oh, you have fabulous taste.

Although 12 years old may seem a little young to be publishing a memoir, that makes me a grande dame in dog years, so I figured it was time to tell all. If we've already met on the internet, *salut*. It's lovely to see you offscreen and on these pages. If this is our first time meeting, *bienvenue*. I'm so grateful you're coming along for the ride.

I'm known as a gay icon and a small (but mighty) fashionista, but that is only scratching the surface. I contain multitudes. Within these pages you'll find never-before-seen photos of some of my favorite sartorial choices, as well as my musings and wisdom on everything from handling the pressure of fame to travel tips and tricks, and, of course, fashion advice. If you've ever wondered "What would Tika do?", you're in the right place.

My story began just over a decade ago, when my papa Louis brought me home from rural Quebec to Montreal. A year later he met my future dad, Thomas, who loved to take pictures of me. Six years later they were married—I was a beautiful maid of honor, obviously—and now my family has expanded to include a baby brother and sister, too.

But enough about the humans. My name is Tika, I'm an Italian greyhound, and I weigh 9 lb (4 kg). My sun is in Cancer (ambitious, compassionate, and goofy), and

I love to snack. I'm an entrepreneur, fashionista, poet, cucumber enthusiast, and human-rights advocate, and I still get more than 20 hours of sleep per day. With my sleep schedule you'd be forgiven for assuming that I just awoke one morning and found out that I was a star, but I'm no stranger to the hustle.

While I enjoy lounging in the nude from time to time (especially in a sunny spot), I gravitate toward fuzzy blankets and cozy couture. Comfort always comes first. It can get quite cold here in Montreal, so my love of fashion isn't only whimsical, it's practical. From a statement collar to my booties, I don't miss an opportunity to express myself through couture. The dog park is a venue to show off both my speed and my accessories.

Once my dad began documenting bits and pieces of my life online, we learned that I wasn't the only one who appreciated my penchant for a faux-fur jacket or flouncy gown. With my humble nature it hasn't been hard to stay grounded. It also helps that I'm a little lady on four legs—never too far from the ground! Whether I'm saying hello to a neighbor at home or meeting celebrities in the Big Apple, you'll always see my tail wag.

As my following grew online, so did the opportunities in real life. I've been fortunate enough to sit front row at Fashion Week in New York, Paris, and Milan, attend a Broadway show and strut down the runway at Vancouver Fashion Week (I think I was a natural). I've collaborated with iconic fashion houses Valentino, Fendi, Christian Siriano, Boss, Moschino, and other luxury brands. I've been featured in *Vogue*, *Cosmopolitan*, and *People* magazine, and starred in a nationwide TV commercial. It's also been a thrill to make new friends who understand my famous lifestyle, such as Whoopi Goldberg, Drew Barrymore, and Kristen Bell.

Most importantly, my growing platform has allowed me to lend my voice to important causes. As a self-proclaimed gay icon, my online presence has always been about providing a pawsitive space and promoting self-expression. I am grateful to be able to advocate for causes that are important to me—with great power comes great responsibility, after all.

I may be small, but that doesn't mean I can't make a big impact. You'll see.

Bisous!

Notes from a

FASHION
ICON

While my fashion journey began for purely practical reasons—do you know how cold it can get in Montreal?—I quickly fell in love with the way fashion allowed me to express myself everywhere from the runway to my favorite fire hydrant. As a sleek lady with very little fur, cozy is my first priority. And although wearing clothes came very naturally to me (not something all my pooch pals relate to, I know), modeling those outfits requires turning things up a notch.

My most important piece of beauty advice? Get that beauty rest and hydrate, hydrate, hydrate. I aim for about 20 hours of sleep per day, but power naps will do if you can't squeeze in that much. After gracing the covers of magazines and participating in fashion weeks around the world, I've picked up a few more practical tips and tricks to keep up my puffy sleeve. A magician may never reveal their tricks, but a generous fashionista certainly does. Follow me down the runway to become best in show.

Power posing

As an Instagram star, I've obviously been in front of the camera for a long time, but it can take some getting used to. The most important thing is confidence. If it isn't coming naturally, it is something you can practice, I promise. The old adage "fake it 'til you make it" certainly applies here, so if you find you typically slouch or look like you're shrinking from the camera, it's time to shake off that self-doubt and practice standing tall (whether you're a quadruped or a biped) until it's second nature.

Posture is everything. Shoulders back and chin up, babies. Keep those paws firmly grounded and draw strength from your tail to the top of your head to be solid in your power stances. Find photo references of models and poses that speak to you, and try to emulate them in front of your mirror at home before you even bring a camera or photographer into the mix. (If you're self-conscious about posing for someone else, might I suggest a tripod and self-timer? Sisters doing it for themselves.)

I've been told that my facial expressions are limited (I do have to respectfully disagree; have you seen my smiley snoot?), but there's no reason why you can't mix things up. Serve face! Puckery pouts, big laughs (we all love a mid-laugh "candid" shot), and sultry stares can totally change the vibe of a shoot, so don't be afraid to have a wide repertoire of faces to pull. Feel silly? That's normal when you're not used to having a lens pointed at you all the time, but you can practice this too. Think of it as a drama masterclass in front of your own mirror. Next thing you know you'll be a pro in front of the camera—and maybe even ready to be scouted by a hot Broadway agent. (This is what I'm banking on. I've got *at least* 36 expressions. Someone get me onstage!)

My satiny snoot looks great no matter what angle it's captured from, and that's because every angle is a good one as long as you're feeling it. While you may believe that you have a "good side" in pictures, I'm here to tell you that from right and left, up and down, you're gorgeous, hunnies. That said, make sure you're comfortable on set.

Right and left, up and down,

you're gorgeous, hunnies.

Speak up if you're not happy with a direction or concept. If I'm not into a shoot, I'll hold out until it goes my way, or at least until I get a treat out of it. Diva behavior? Not in my opinion. It's called knowing your own worth.

I like to incorporate some organic movement into my shoots. Being a statuesque four-legged model means that I like to highlight my silvery gams. Whether your forte is sitting pretty or rolling over, it's great to be a model who is comfortable to do more than park and bark. Let your personality shine through. This is also a great way to incorporate props to inject natural movement and character into your photos. I haven't been able to master hula hooping, sadly, but I think that could look cool for you, somehow.

You can also add levels to your photo shoots by incorporating furniture into the set and switching up your poses. I like to show off my pretty paws by putting my feet up on the table like a lady, or leaning casually out of a New York taxi. And if there's an element of your outfit that you want to highlight—a glitzy collar or fanciful fringe, for example—make sure you're posing to pull focus accordingly. Whatever you do, you better werk, bitch!

Confidence will shine through in any photo, whether it's a selfie or an editorial. Having treats on hand to keep you focused (and perhaps to use as a focal point for my fellow canine models) is also helpful. Love yourself and your selfie. When you're feeling it, you'll be into the shutter snapping, too.

A perfect fit

In a world where trend cycles feel ever quicker, it can be easy to get caught up in a whirlwind of fast fashion, but there is a reason why quintessential looks come back season after season. Trends come and go, but classics are forever. You'll never have to worry about keeping up with the latest fashions if you invest in some key timeless pieces.

By having a capsule of essential staples in your wardrobe, you'll be able to nail maximal sartorial effect with minimal effort—the dream! Plus, on days when picking out an outfit is less enticing than a trip to the vet, you'll be able to fall back on looks that are tried, true, and you. My essentials include a chic tan trench coat, my coziest faux-fur jacket, a sleek black turtleneck, and a cheerfully bright set of matching loungewear. To get the most out of investment pieces, don't settle for an "almost" perfect fit—become besties with your local tailor. As a model with a fairly niche body type, I know the importance of custom tailoring. When the outfit is snug in all the right places, it's just *chef's kiss*.

Speaking of trends, athleisure has proven that it's here to stay, and I'm here for that. The key to pulling off this look is to ensure that there is some element of structure, coordination, and polish to your ensemble. A tapered leg on a tracksuit really does it for me—we're acing that serve, even if I don't make it to a tennis court. A well-cut athleisure outfit proves that there is no reason to sacrifice style for comfort, and vice versa. We really can have it all.

If ever you feel overwhelmed by choice, or wish you could just wear your favorite outfit all the time, there is

something to be said for a uniform. There's a reason why so many successful people stick to a signature style or even a specific outfit. Although I personally love switching things up too much ever to give up the variety of getting dressed fabulously every day, I can see the appeal.

For some, a signature style might be a pair of black trousers and a crisp white shirt; for others, it might be a fleece stegosaurus onesie. There is no wrong answer if it's a look that you are happy to pull off time and time again. Besides, there's nothing bad about having a look that people associate with you. Bonus points if you can get your squad into your uniform, too.

On that note, I am a big proponent of repeating outfits. Why should an #OOTD get just one day to shine? So many hours go into the creation of each custom design, and every photo shoot and runway is an opportunity to show off the work of the incredible designers I have the privilege to collaborate with. It would be a shame to wear a beautiful gown only once, so I like to repeat. Plus, it's better for the planet to recycle your outfits and give them a long life. Sustainability? *Très chic.*

More than a fashion statement, your outfit can make a political statement, too. As a gay icon, I am proud to strut around town in my rainbow outfits and wear my heart on my sleeve.

Wear the rainbow

Color your world! Yes, black goes with everything, but a pop of color can brighten everyone's day. Find a palette that makes you happy, and you'll pass any test with flying colors. If kaleidoscopic hues make you dizzy, don't doubt the power of a monochromatic moment. Committing to a single color can make quite the impact. Go for different shades of the same color for a kind of ombre effect, or stick to a single hue. One and done. Effortless. We love it.

Or—make a splash with a clash. If it sounds as though I'm contradicting myself, that's because fashion rules are made to be broken. Be bold. The days of shying away from more than one pattern or print in an outfit are long gone, so mix and match to your heart's content. Polka dots, plaid, stripes—I'm here for them all, and sometimes all at once. Subtlety isn't the name of the game when we're rocking highlighter hues. I am meant to stand out and so are you, honey.

Maximalism, minimalism— and everything in between

Am I a maximalist? Some days. Am I a minimalist? Also, yes. We all contain multitudes, so don't let anyone put you in a box. Who says you can't be a fashionista who rocks a denim tuxedo *and* a baby-pink tutu? One day I may be the most extra Italian greyhound you cross paths with, and the next I feel ready to leave the house wearing only a dainty collar. I don't subscribe to labels when it comes to my personal style. I'm a proponent of feel-good fashion— however that looks for you.

When it comes to maximalism, I love elevating an outfit with statement accessories. The smallest details can take a look in a completely different direction. There

is also something delightful about accessories that seem impractical (although, of course, if they're part of a look I'd argue that they *are* practical). What do I keep in my teeny-tiny purses? Huge secrets (and a snack).

My own hair is short and smooth, so I love to punch things up by playing with textural textiles in my outfits: fringe, frills, feathers—anything to add dimension and sculptural interest to my tiny frame. I also like to borrow from my animal cousins when it comes to fashion inspiration. From the farm to the savannah, this dog can change her spots and stripes wherever, whenever. The only fur I wear is faux, of course. Take back your mink!

Everyone knows that diamonds are a girl's best friend. I'm also very good friends with sequins, glitter, pearls ... and jewels of any kind, let's be honest. Bedazzled and bewitching is a beautiful combo. But don't limit the sparkle to formalwear or jewelry. A little shabby-chic moment is always a fun way to dress something up or down, and a strategic sequined patch can make any outfit party-ready.

Up the drama with some volume—the more ruffles the better, as far as I'm concerned. I don't love being in the water, but I do love swimming in flounces, puffy sleeves, and tulle.

When you've pulled together an outfit you love, don't forget to top it off with a flourish. Put your thinking cap on; traditional hats are great, but get creative and think of all the pom-poms, tiaras, and butterflies you can wear up there, too. Ear muffs are another perfect accessory for the cold—and for making sure you don't listen to any negativity out there.

Remember, if you think something is too much ... no, it's not. More is more and less is a bore.

Runway-ready

Why some folks call it a catwalk, I will never know. The runway was made for canines. Again, confidence is the key here. Putting your best paw forward becomes easier with practice, practice, practice.

Once you've made your stylistic choices, there are some tricks to keep up your sleeve as you practice your little turn on the runway. First, get in the mood. Find the bops that make you want to put the bass in your walk and practice that strut. Everyone has a pump-up song or playlist that revs them up for the task at hand. Mine? The entirety of Céline Dion's discography. Once you know which tracks get you in the modeling mood, keep that playlist on hand to give you a mindset boost.

Next, think tall. I may not stand much more than 15 in (38 cm) off the ground, but with my head held high no one questions my stature on the runway. Keep an assured sass in your step, and don't forget your power poses. Hold each one for a beat longer than you think necessary. There's no rush, and you don't want folks to miss taking all of your look in.

Finally, find your light. Don't search for the spotlight; be so alluring that it finds you. If you feel you're walking into a blinding glare, remember to fix your gaze on a focal point and keep your eyes up. Eye contact is a strong indicator of confidence, so work on that smize and look straight at the cameras. Say cheese! (Maybe only internally.)

Runway practice is also the perfect opportunity to test outfits that are outside your comfort zone, and to create your own fancy-dress occasions. If your favorite pieces are collecting dust, consider this your cue to glam it up for your next trip to the dog park (or the convenience store, the couch, the cafe ... you get the idea). There is no reason too small to feel fabulous.

If you love something you *can* wear it. Don't put off feeling your best just because the perfect occasion isn't in your social calendar (yet). Dress for the life you want, and celebrate what makes you feel best. For me, that can be anything from a tapered tracksuit to a dramatic peacock ensemble. Variety is the spice of life, after all. Dress like every day is Friday. Every hour is happy hour. The world is our oyster.

Rain on me, tsunami

Some people like to say that there's no such thing as bad weather, only bad clothing. Well, those people are obviously not nine-pound dogs who hate the cold. I can't avoid all that Mother Nature throws at us, so I like to be prepared. Faux fur, layers of fleece, and warm wool are some of my favorite ways to brave the cold. You'll never catch me outside on a winter's day without my snood. This stylish staple keeps my delicate neck and perfect ears in a cozy tube of warmth. In Montreal it can be freezing one day and balmy the next, so I'm a big fan of layers and transitional outerwear. Never be caught unprepared, bbs!

I'm much happier when I can soak up the sun, and I get my best snoozes in sunny patches. But there is nothing less fashionable than a sunburn, and yes, I can get them too (but I don't, because I am always prepared with sun

protection). Remember that every body is a beach body, just don't forget the SPF while you're soaking up the sun. I protect my soft pink belly with classic swimwear, and my snoot avoids catching those UV rays with a brimmed sun hat. A dramatic pair of sunglasses is also a must—plus it comes in handy when you need to hide from the paparazzi.

I am extremely well prepared for everyone's favorite micro-season: those days when just a sweater will do to keep you snug in the crisp autumn air. Better than any pumpkin spice latte, good-quality knitwear can be dressed up or down. From a walk in the park to a ritzy cafe, you know I'm a well-stitched bitch.

Commit to the bit

Embrace a theme! Go all out for a party! Accept dress codes as a challenge! Halloween? You know I'm dressing up. A holiday party? I make a perfect reindeer. Florals for spring? Groundbreaking. Going over the top? There's no such thing.

Whether it be cottagecore, coastal grandma, or boho chic, playing with sartorial trends doesn't mean you need to shop for a new wardrobe. Play with pieces you own and shop your own closet to keep things fresh and fun. For example, I love to dress the part when I get out of the city. At a cottage, expect me to lean into the aesthetic: a little kitschy, a lot cute, and with a crown of wild flowers.

Although I do delight in being a muse, I am moved by so many people and so much art that I also love to reference the greats. From movie stars to songstress queens, there are so many iconic fashion moments to emulate that I'm never short on inspiration. Always be referencing.

Charisma, uniqueness

When I'm very relaxed, sometimes my tongue slips out for the camera. My snaggle tooth might make an appearance, and we're all here for it. Cherish what makes you unique, flaws and all. It's a universal truth: you can't please everyone and you shouldn't try. Some people may feel the need to voice their unkind thoughts about you (shockingly, I have some experience in this arena), but you don't have to give them your time or energy. Haters gonna hate, and, as they say, shake it off. (More about this in chapter 5.) Life is a lot more fun when you're able to be unapologetically yourself. Don't let others dictate how you present yourself to the world—dress for yourself.

Feeling good and looking good are like a positive feedback loop—one encourages the other. So spread that pawsitivity to others as often as you can. Sprinkle compliments around like confetti. It might be a dog-eat-dog world out there, but it is so easy to spread a little joy and tell someone you love their new collar. Collaboration is greater than competition, and kindness looks good on everyone. We've all got it, so be sure to flaunt it.

CHAPTER ONE

Sip on
AN ITALIAN GREYHOUND

It just feels classy to have a go-to libation. Some ladies have their cosmopolitans, 007 has his martini, and those in the know have an Italian Greyhound. I can't claim that this cocktail was created in my honor, since it's been around for decades, but I like to think that anyone ordering one these days is thinking of me.

To make your own Italian Greyhound, simply pour 1½ fl oz (40 ml) vodka, ½ fl oz (15 ml) Campari, and 5 fl oz (150 ml) freshly squeezed grapefruit juice into a glass. Fill up with ice and stir to combine. Garnish with a fresh slice of grapefruit. If you'd like to add your own twist, try a salted rim, a herb-infused simple syrup (I'd recommend rosemary for a wintry flavor combo), or swap the Campari out for Aperol.

However you enjoy it,

cin cin!

Tika gets

IN-
VOLVED

may be teeny-tiny, but that doesn't mean I can't make a big impact. Each of us has a part to play in bettering our communities, both online and IRL. My online home has always been a place to showcase canine creativity, a little silliness, and a lot of fashionable fun, and from the start it's been equally important to me that it be a pawsitive and inclusive space for everyone who stops by.

The internet is a big place, and there is a lot out there to prey on our insecurities, anxieties, and fears. I've always been on a mission to bring joy to my little corner of the World Wide Web, and part of that joy includes working to use my platform for good. Whether it be a collaboration with a charitable campaign, sharing educational resources online, or simply lending my pretty face to a good cause, I'm of the mind that every effort is valuable, and each bit of good counts. If you think your platform is too small, or that your good deeds go unnoticed, just think of all the expressions humans use about the ripple effect of positivity, the power of a single mosquito, the strength of a bundle of twigs as opposed to a twig on its lonesome, and so on—all clichés, maybe, but all true. We're stronger together, and each little bit adds up. Any act of kindness, no matter how small, gets a big tail wag from me.

A gay icon

You can't spell "gay icon" without LGBTIKA! My fans began calling me a gay icon because I have two dads and wear fabulous outfits, but given my platform and voice, it's important for me to give back to my community. I'm an advocate by choice, but also simply by virtue of the way I exist. Sometimes being "political" or landing in activism isn't a choice. By being proudly open about having a loving family that happens to have two dads, I can't help but loudly voice my support for the LGBTQIA2+ communities. Love is love, after all.

Being a gay icon certainly comes with responsibility, but it was a natural fit as my platform grew. I often hear from people who say that my photos and videos brighten their days, and have even allowed them to come out for the first time or lighten difficult conversations with some Tika-levity. It is an honor to be able to help in this way, and a reminder to never doubt the power of your platform. I am inspired by all the amazing, outspoken artists and activists who paved the way for a hound like me to be able to prance around in my best rainbow attire, and aspire to help others as much as I can while I have your ear.

Follow the Rainbow Railroad

If you're keen to get involved in activist spaces but unsure about where to begin, look inward and think about what kind of work or cause really resonates with you. One of the nonprofits I'm most passionate about partnering with is Rainbow Railroad. They work globally to help LGBTQIA2+ people facing persecution based on their sexual orientation and/or gender identity. While I'm so grateful that my hometown of Montreal is generally a safe and wonderful city for people to love whoever they love, that isn't the case in many other places around the world. Queer people are especially vulnerable to harm caused by systemic, state-enabled homophobia and transphobia, which leads to them either being displaced in their own country, or unable to escape harm and migrate to somewhere safe. Since its inception, Rainbow Railroad has helped thousands of LGBTQIA2+ people find safety. You can learn more about its life-changing work at rainbowrailroad.org.

Although I'm unable to get my paws on the ground and actually physically help these people, I've raised funds for the cause through sales of my (very cute) merch and through my closet sales, and have amplified Rainbow Railroad's important work on my account. Everybody has skills or attributes to help others, so even (especially?) if you're not an Instagram Italian greyhound model, never doubt that you have exactly what you need to help. On top of this, one of the great things about volunteering is that it allows you to hone your talents and gain new ones. (And not that I dream of labor, but you never know which skills may land you a future gig or dream job.)

Begin before you're ready

If we all waited until we knew everything before hopping to action, we'd never get started. The best time to begin is now. Don't be afraid to get involved; we all have to start somewhere. If you think you don't know enough to be helpful, you're wrong. Besides, you can always learn as you go.

There are so many resources at the tips of our paws these days that it's easy to do your own research if you're just dipping your paws into a space. From there, find the people who inspire you in whatever space you're working in, and follow their lead. You may find a lifelong mentor, or become a mentor to someone else. While continuing education is always a good thing, don't get so caught up in the theory that you forget to take action. (My advice is full of paradoxes.) Reading *is* fundamental, but we can't always have our snoots in books.

Be ambitious, but be sure to set realistic goals. When you're working on things you care about, it's easy to find a sense of purpose, and you don't want to set yourself up for disappointment by choosing goals that are too broad. This can leave you feeling that you're barking up the wrong tree. For example, it might feel overwhelming to think about activism around climate change. Where to start? "Stop the climate crisis" (yes, please!) is a very good and lofty goal, but it may be better to approach it in a way that allows you to celebrate smaller, but still important, wins. A classic way to frame this breakdown is to think globally but act locally. If your mission is climate action, why not see what you can do in your local community? I've been known to show up at a climate strike or two, and there are always park cleanups to be done. Get in touch with your local representatives to let them know that you care about strong climate policies. Push for more accessible greenspace for canines and humans. Help with local habitat conservation. Contribute to a community garden. Plant a tree. I'll cheer you on!

Furry friends

I would hope that this is obvious, but a cause *very* near and dear to my heart is animal welfare. (And I would also hope that it's obvious that any "fur" you see me sporting is definitely faux … except for my own silky coat, of course.)

I was the smallest whippersnapper of my litter, and I'm so grateful that I was adopted into a loving home where I've truly been able to live my best life. That's what I want for every pup. If you're thinking of adding a furry friend to your family, I would encourage you to check your local animal shelter or foster agencies as a starting point. Don't overlook the rescues and the senior dogs who could thrive with a little TLC. And next time you see a bake sale in support of my fellow party animals, don't forget to pick me up a treat, too.

Stay humble

If you're just learning about an issue or cause: listen. Remember that we're all on lifelong learning journeys. Be open to learning new things, discovering new perspectives, and hearing about the life experiences of others. Especially if you're engaging in work or communities where you're in a position of privilege, acknowledge your privilege and be a good ally by listening and taking cues from those with less of it (while being aware of the relative nature of this privilege based on the intersections of gender, race, class, and so on). Not everyone understands the trials

Any act of kindness, no matter how small, gets a big tail wag from me.

and tribulations of an iggy, and that's OK. I'm here for questions.

In the same vein, know that everyone makes mistakes, and that's fine. I know I've committed the occasional sartorial sin, but I learn from my errors. As long as we commit to growth and humbly accept that we'll stumble from time to time, mistakes are all part of the process. Once you're a seasoned veteran in your activist circles, don't forget to give the same grace you were given to newcomers. Be patient and helpful; building movements depends on getting the next generation(s) involved, too. Set a good example, and others can follow in your pawprints.

Don't begin volunteering your time expecting anything in return—we're talking altruism, honey! But if you're lucky, you'll find the benefits of helping others to be many: among them learning opportunities, new friends, and making a tangible difference in ways that matter to you. At a time when it's easy to feel anxiety and despair at the state of many things, I find that helping where I can is a lovely antidote to feeling helpless and cynical. Hope is contagious, so spread it wherever you go.

Activate joy

While resistance and pushing for change can certainly be grueling and potentially dangerous work, don't forget that joy is a key part of activism as well. By finding joy in your activism you'll be able to connect to your passions, stay focused, avoid burnout, and have fun along the way. Don't underestimate the power of community care as self-care. I'm the first to admit that I love a cushy night in with no obligations, but sometimes getting out and contributing to a team effort on some kind of project and progress fills my cup better than anything else.

Rope your friends into the fun, too. The more the merrier, especially when it comes to bettering the world. Trying to get your pals to join a rally? Bribe them with brunch afterward if you must. You never know who you may inspire to take up the cause. (I will say, ensuring that cute dogs can participate is always a good draw.)

Lead with love, bring joy to your work, and remember to have fun. Getting involved in causes that matter to you helps to give you a sense of purpose, connects you to your community and like-minded people, and will likely give you the warm and fuzzies (not to mention good karma). As long as you're making the world a better place, get that serotonin boost we can all use from doing something good.

Hallelu.

CHAPTER 3

TRAVEL

with Tika

'm known to sniff out adventure wherever I go, and I've been lucky to have many opportunities to get my pawsport stamped over the years. Although I like to think of myself as a low-maintenance lady, I do recognize that enjoying my presence while traveling does require a little (worthwhile) extra planning. From cosmopolitan city centers to quiet countryside, I have a suitcase full of travel tips for any destination.

The Grand Hotel

Whether it's a staycation or a big trip, a good hotel is my favorite kind of home away from home. The little luxuries, the plush bathrobe, room service, a knowledgeable concierge—I can't get enough! Take advantage of whatever perks your accommodation has to offer. A room with a view? Yes, please. Complimentary breakfast? I want to go to there. Are there upgrades? I would like them all.

Not all hotels are properly equipped to cater for four-legged guests, so it's important to do your homework to ensure that you have the most sumptuous stay possible. Find out ahead of time what the hotel's policies are for VIP canine guests. If your human travel companions plan on giving you some quality alone time in the hotel, make sure you've traveled with the essentials you need for solo time at home. Some hotels even offer doggy daycare or walking services, should you need a little extra pampering while you're there.

I love boutique and *historique* hotels alike—in both cases, they are more than simply locations to rest my weary head at the end of a long day of travel or exploration. I like to make sure I have time to enjoy all the amenities on offer, whether it's stately lobbies with stunning artwork or a refreshing cucumber water at a swanky hotel bar. A hotel backdrop is also the perfect setting to live out my Wes Anderson-style cinematic dreams. Catch me in whimsical silk pajamas, dramatic organza, or, of course, my personalized bathrobe. I'm always ready to check in.

Tika go lightly

For my dads, I *am* a carry-on item! But of course I need my own bag, too—no one would expect a fashion icon to travel without a handful of costume changes, would they? As a rule, we avoid checking luggage as often as possible. Flying through security before you take to the skies makes navigating airports a breeze, and we also get to avoid waiting at the luggage carousel at our destination. I've become a very efficient packer, as I have to be ready for all occasions. Whether I have a meet and greet or a photo shoot or am strolling around a new city, I always love to look and feel my best.

I may be small, but my wardrobe certainly isn't, and sometimes it's tricky to pare down. Every piece is my favorite! I've learned that it's well worth taking the time to lay out every single item I'm thinking of bringing with me, and planning out each day's outfits. We're visual learners in my household, so this entails physically laying out each item to be packed and deciding from there, but I have heard that some people get away with simply making a list. If "packing" turns into "impromptu fashion show," so be it—whatever helps with the process. By planning each day's outfit ahead I'm able to eliminate superfluous pieces from my suitcase, and quickly be ready for each day while I'm on the go. That means less time worrying in front of the mirror, and more time to explore (although I always find time to admire my own looks, of course). Another advantage of packing lightly? There's room in my bag for souvenirs. Plus, if I happen to forget something, I'm never mad to have an excuse for a quick shopping trip. All of that said, you never know when you'll want to wear your organza floral appliqué gown—sometimes a fashionista just has to pack her favorite extravagance. Let's be real, my dads will be carrying my luggage, so I can relax.

Now, I normally avoid any clothing items with the words "technical" or "gear" in their description (ew), but sometimes a lady has to be prepared for specific adventures. My coyote vest doesn't just make a statement (although it certainly does that—neon! spikes! spaghetti?), but it also keeps me from becoming prey for larger animals I may encounter on my travels to more remote locations. Sometimes you really do need a specific piece of ... technical gear. And when you do, it's best to splurge on safety.

To help make packing less of a chore, I like to keep a small bag at the ready so that some basic essentials are always in the same spot when it's time to jet. Think passport, favorite leash, treats, and a pee pad. Good to go!

Planes, trains, and automobiles

While shaking things up is fun, I know most pets do best when we stick to our routines. That's why my dads try to plan any flights or longer rail and road rides during my typical mealtimes. That way, I'm happily eating while we're en route, and less apt to notice anything stressful about my changing environment.

A great way to ensure that your furry friend has a pleasant journey is to make sure they're comfortable in the carrier. It's their home on the road, after all. I'm such a fan of mine that I like to snooze in there when I'm at home, and on trips it's kitted out with one of my favorite blankies for optimal snoozing. Napping on the way to a destination? That's what I call multitasking. Take that as a cue to travel with whatever you need to help you keep up with your beauty rest. Whether that means bringing your cooling eye mask, noise-canceling headphones, or favorite tea, set yourself up for sleepy success.

I'm a thirsty gal, and that only increases when I'm on the go. If I'm not going to be near my water bowl, my dads always have a collapsible bowl and a reusable water bottle on hand to keep me from being parched. This tongue needs to stay moisturized.

I don't usually get to hear my dads' travel playlists if we're on a plane or train, but if it's a family road trip then I absolutely have requests for the car DJ: queen Celine's greatest hits, Shania Twain, and the latest Lizzo, please.

I may be small, but my wardrobe certainly isn't.

Planned spontaneity

Ooh, I do love a good travel wish list: things to see, restaurants not to miss, events in town, and the best spots for a golden-hour photo shoot. I fully endorse preparing maps with pins ahead of time, and a spreadsheet with my detailed itinerary makes me feel organized and in control. Researching before a trip is all part of the joy of travel. I'm not much for FOMO, but I do hate the thought of missing out on something amazing at my destination just because I didn't take the time to plan.

However, I have learned to accept that I can't do everything or be everywhere all at once. It's great to be prepared, but especially as I get older I like to leave some unstructured time in any itinerary to give myself the flexibility to tack on unexpected fun. Whether it's meeting new travel friends, a last-minute invitation to a glamorous after-party, or just making another detour to the cafe with the best dog biscuits, you never know what might come up. A flexible itinerary can also allow you to slow down for a scenic route, and wander off the beaten path. Plan for spontaneity; even if it just leaves you with time for a nap you didn't know you needed, you won't regret it.

Adventures in your own backyard

One doesn't have to go far for a change of scenery. Even when I'm staying close to home, there are always new things to see and sniff. Change up the daily dog-walk route, check out a new park, inspect a new boutique?

Mais oui. Playing tourist close to home also allows me to support local businesses and entrepreneurs, and that's something I like to do wherever I am in the world. I love connecting with the actual people behind some of my favorite cafes, doggy boutiques, and local attractions.

Leave the passport at home and find adventures in your own backyard. The bonus is that you get to come back to your favorite bed at the end of the day, and have your entire wardrobe at your paws. For more on this, see chapter 6.

When in Rome

... do as the locals do. One of the great things about being so connected to my community online is that I am bound to know a local expert for almost anywhere in the world. A local's perspective is priceless, and I'm always thrilled when people want to share their favorite things about their hometown with me. To connect with locals, don't be afraid to veer away from the guidebook and every "top ten" list out there.

I'm lucky to be a walking conversation-starter, but don't be afraid to chat with the people you meet as you travel. (I'm also lucky to speak a universal language, but I do always encourage my dads to pick up some key phrases of the local language for this purpose.) My goal is always to be the friendliest iggy you'll ever meet, and that doesn't change when I'm away from home. I love making friends with cab drivers, metro riders, and everyone in between—someone may have a hidden gem to tell you about, or you may meet a new lifelong friend. It's all part of the adventure.

I may come across as a material girl, but I'd rather collect experiences than things. If you want to make the most of a trip with a canine companion, look into all the dog-friendly destinations on your journey. Bountiful outdoor locations are always promising, but you might be surprised to find plenty of other spaces where my kind are welcome. I've browsed bookstores and art galleries, and even enjoyed a Broadway show. You'll never know if you don't ask.

Although I always travel with an entourage (it's a mutually beneficial arrangement), there's no reason to hold off on a trip while you wait for a travel buddy's schedule to line up with yours. Don't be afraid to go alone; just remember to let people know where you are going and how to reach you—safety first! Whether you're traveling solo or with a group, trust your instinct. I never doubt my snoot or my gut. I like to try everything twice, but I also like to keep my stress levels down, so if something feels off I'm always happy to bow out and go chill at the nearest dog park.

Dear diary

Sometimes the best souvenir from a trip is a travel journal. There are no rules when it comes to the format—it could be flowery prose on lined pages, or captain's log-style in the notes app on your phone—but I guarantee you'll appreciate having a record of your journey. A photo

record is also a great way to document your trip. A picture is worth a thousand words, after all. So sure, do it for the gram—but also for your memoir.

While you're in writing mood, send your friends postcards. Everyone loves snail mail (and receiving my famous pawprint). Sign any guest books you encounter on your trip with a note of gratitude. Leave kind reviews online for the places you enjoy along the way. It's a free way to give a boost to folks and businesses working in tourism, and I like to pay the love forward. Everyone can use some good karma while traveling, right?

WHAT'S YOUR *sign?*

I'm a Cancer sun, and my birthday is on July 10 if you'd like to mark it on your calendar. This explains why I can't hide my true feelings. As a water sign, Cancers tend to be emotional, and you'll always have a pretty easy time telling how I'm feeling by my body language. Cancers are also stereotypically loyal, homebodies, and ambitious. It all checks out!

Whenever I'm feeling uninspired or stuck in a rut, I like to consult my horoscope for the day. Although we are, of course, far more than our star signs, you never know what nugget of wisdom from your horoscope may prompt some good introspection or a burst of creativity. Take what you need and leave what you don't.

Miss Tika:

HOSTESS

with the

MOSTESS

Sharing is caring, and what could be more caring of me than sharing my time with my nearest and dearest? I love to play hostess and hold court with my fans, I mean, my friends and family (who also happen to be my fans, let's be honest). Being the host means that I get to call the shots and be in charge ... and that I don't have to leave my home, with my favorite spots for napping. Plus, it's a lovely opportunity to get dressed up in my fanciest loungewear. There's nothing like a matching silk pajama set and some statement jewelry to say *"Bienvenue, mes chéries!"*

Hosting events "just because" is a great way to add celebrations in your life without having to wait for milestones such as birthdays or weddings. Have a puppy picnic because your friend is fostering a new dog, have a cocktail party with friends after you've filed taxes, organize a potluck of snacks to gather for your favorite TV show. Once you start looking for things to celebrate, it will be hard to stop! I love impromptu hangouts and always like to be well stocked with dehydrated chicken bites and fresh cucumber so that I'm ready when friends swing by, but there's something to be said for planning something slightly more involved.

If you make the planning part of the fun, there's no need for stress. You don't need to be Martha Stewart to throw a dinner party, and you don't need to break the bank to host a shindig that will be talked about for years to come. With just a little foresight and some thoughtful touches, we can all be a hostess with the mostess.

Break the ice

How much does an Italian greyhound weigh? Enough to break the ice! Well, it depends what kind of ice sheet we're talking about, but in social situations you better believe that I'm equipped to make sure strangers become friends. I always have strategies up my ruffled sleeve to ensure that introductions get off to a good start.

With perpetually busy schedules and only so many waking hours (like, five) in a day for socializing, I like to blend my social groups to maximize gatherings and be able to see all my friends in one go. It can sometimes be nerve-wracking to be in charge of orchestrating this kind of mingling, but it's very rewarding to see my friends become close with one another. After all, they all have me in common, and I have great taste. There are a few things you can do as the host to make sure everyone is as excited as I am about meeting new people:

- *Start before the event.* Whether it's through an email invitation or a group chat, don't doubt the power of a funny meme or some quick virtual introductions to help people connect offline.
- *Embrace the role of the connector.* It's like matchmaking, but with lower romantic stakes (and potentially higher reward). Introduce people with thoughtful details (such as "This is Mark Darcy. Mark's a top barrister"), and highlight things people may have in common, to jump-start their subsequent small talk (such as "You two both love Italian greyhounds"). A considerate

introduction will help to put your pals at ease, and encourage easier conversation among them.

- *Game on.* A group activity or social game will encourage new friends to team up and work toward a common goal. A little competition always helps to warm things up and get the laughs going. Take a hint from *Drag Race* and have your guests lip-sync for their lives, or keep things chill and simply have guests guess how many dog treats are in the jar. (The winner gets to hand me my treat.) It doesn't have to be competitive—perhaps host a group cooking class so that everyone gets to take part in making dinner.

- *Step back and relax.* You can only do so much. If your friends hit it off, fabulous! If they don't seem keen to engage beyond small talk, let them do their thing. Don't take it personally.

I try to set my party guests up for success, then I just make sure that I'm having fun, too. At the very least, they can always default to discussing whatever fabulous outfit I've chosen to wear that day. Worst-case scenario? They get stuck mingling by the food—doesn't everyone always end up in the kitchen? I know that's where I like to hang out for optimal crumb-finding—and bond over their favorite chip flavor. That leads me to what I think is the most important part of any event ...

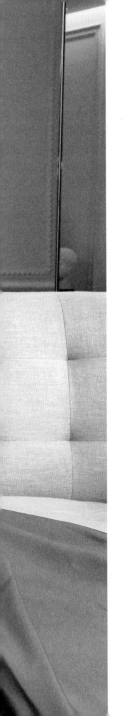

Feasting for fun

Food and drink are an integral part of gatherings and rituals. Can you imagine any significant cultural event without them? I know I'm a much happier guest if I don't have to sit pretty and beg for a snack (although I'm not above doing it if I have to).

As a lady of leisure, and not much of a cook myself, I always suggest that a host consider catering. Support a favorite local restaurant or caterer, and let the professionals do the heavy lifting to satiate your guests. Whether it's a brunch spread of bagels and lox, oysters on the half-shell with bubbly, or a three-course meal, I'm happy to leave the culinary creativity to the experts.

If I am in charge of snacks, I like to keep things simple and serve my favorites: finely diced fresh fruit and vegetables (I particularly love watermelon and cucumber), and unseasoned chicken breasts. Yum! (Now do you see why I love caterers?)

A potluck is a fun way to get your guests involved in the meal planning and preparation. It opens up your menu to more creativity and is a nice way to sit down to a filling meal without leaving the entire bill to the host. I'm always sure to touch base with the group ahead of time to sort out at least a general menu plan, lest everyone try to be my favorite by bringing their best platter of sliced cucumber.

For those of you who insist on wowing your guests with your prowess in the kitchen, it's a great idea to prep as much as you can ahead of your event. My second favorite dad's mother likes to boast that she aims to be *so* prepared before a dinner party that in the half-hour

before her guests arrive she can sit down and relax with a book (who is she?). Short of that level of organization, any food prep you can get out of the way in the day(s) before the gathering will help you be that much more relaxed come party time. Unless you're comfortable winging it (and have a pizza delivery number on hand for backup), a dinner party isn't the time to experiment with a new-to-you recipe. In general, you want to cut down on uncertainties and potential stress when you're hosting, so serving dishes that you are already comfortable making is your best bet. If you need me to come over and sample your cooking beforehand, just let me know.

No matter where your food is coming from, be sure to account for your guests' dietary restrictions. In my family there's a severe nut allergy, a vegan, and the occasional keto/paleo diet, and of course there's a whole list of things I can't eat—but we make it work. Inquiring ahead of time about your guests' allergies and dietary requirements shows that you care and will avoid any awkwardness when you try to serve your lactose-intolerant friend a beautiful cheesy pizza.

Although a chilled bottle of champagne is a traditional go-to for a celebratory libation, my refreshment of choice is cool cucumber-infused water. Don't forget to have delicious non-alcoholic options on hand for drivers and anyone who may not be consuming alcohol for any reason (and remember, they don't need to explain why). Make sure that your guests have a safe way to get home, and have extra fluffy dog pillows around for unexpected sleepovers if need be. Cheers to responsibility!

Great expectations

Along with the regular details, such as time and place, if it's not meant to be a surprise, let your guests know a little about what they should expect when you send your invitation. Is it a movie night in PJs? Will there be a meal? Is it BYOTFT? (The answer to that last one is yes, always bring your own treats for Tika.)

As the host, you get to set the tone, and it starts with the invitation. Is this a casual "Come for dinner—my dads are barbecuing, you bring the cucumber water!" situation, or a more formal "Cocktails will be served at 7pm. Arrive in your chicest silks" kind of thing? (Yes, I suppose there is a middle ground.) Letting your guests in on the plan will help them to arrive relaxed and ready to party.

Queen of clean

Break up the cleaning and chores you have to do in the day(s) leading up to hosting, so that it can be done in manageable, less soul-crushing tasks. If you're able to delegate to another household member or friend, you should. For example, I like to hand the vacuuming to someone else because I can't help but be wary of those robots.

Prioritize your tasks. Yes, I like to make sure my home is presentable before I welcome guests, but I also keep things in perspective. The day of the party is not the time for my dads to finally purge the junk drawer, or organize the bookshelves alphabetically. A tidy and welcoming

Is it BYOTFT?

(The answer is yes, always bring your own treats for Tika.)

space with a fresh pee pad is enough for me. Your guests are coming to have a good time, not to cast a judgmental eye over your home (but if they do that, perhaps they shouldn't be invited next time).

Category is ...

We love a theme. A themed party can add an element of whimsy and fun to your event. It can make for great photos and can even act as a reason for having a party in the first place. Why *not* gather purely because everyone wants to wear their favorite Tika-inspired outfit?

Be it a murder mystery, a costume party, a 1980s aerobics-themed fundraiser, or a wild karaoke night in, commit to whatever theme you pick, from invitations to snacks and decor. The theme can be as abstract or as cliché as you like, and the more you buy in, the more enthusiastic your partygoers will be.

Beware of faux paws

Ultimately, I like to be a hostess *sans souci*—carefree and laid-back. Although it certainly takes a bit of effort to make an event look effortless, remember not to sweat the small stuff. Your guests will remember the fun they had, and how welcome you made them feel—not the fact that I shed a little bit on the couch. Mishaps happen with even the best-laid plans, and a good host rolls with the punches. You may be critical of an overbaked dog biscuit,

but that doesn't mean you need to let your guests in on that self-criticism. Let them enjoy their snacks and each other's company without you dwelling on any details that aren't totally perfect.

Chances are, any mistakes or accidents will be more quickly forgotten by all involved if they are handled with grace and humility. Glasses break, water bowls get flipped on the floor, but the party goes on. You *and* your guests will have way more fun if you're able to relax and enjoy yourself.

There are only a few faux pas that would really make my hair stand on end, and that I'd avoid at all costs:

- Welcoming guests to my abode with a used pee pad— *non merci*! Even casual hangouts deserve a fresh potty patch, I think. And I make sure that my dads give the human bathroom a look over, too.
- Running out of food or drink. I'd always rather have too many treats on hand than not enough (duh!), and there's nothing less fun than realizing you're out of provisions halfway through a party. Ensure that you're well stocked.
- Tidying up while your guests are still enjoying themselves—unless you want them to feel they have to get out of your fur. It's a sure way to kill the mood. That said, it's your party and you can wrap things up when you want to. I have been known to sneak away for a little nap—you know how I love my beauty rest. It's not rude, it's self-care.

- Not being a good neighbor. If your neighbors don't make the guest list, at least be considerate and keep barking to a minimum later in the evening.

Tika's touch

Anyone who knows me knows that I love to be cozy, so I love to curate a space for living and entertaining that is warm and snug. When I'm expecting guests I like to strew extra blankets artfully on the couch, and I'll set out additional dog pillows so that no one can accuse me of hogging mine.

Once you've got the big-ticket items—food, venue, activities—nailed down, have fun with the final touches. This is where you can really solidify the ~vibe~ and the details that seem small can have a big impact. Pick elements of decor to complement the theme if there is one, or just to highlight the loveliness of the season if there isn't. Think local flower arrangements, statement candles, or even decorative gourds (they will never go out of style). A signature mocktail, strings of twinkling lights, and a playlist to match the mood are examples of little things that can take your party to the next level. Send your guests home with doggy bags that include a little treat to remind them of the delightful time you just shared.

While a well-executed party is the stuff my hostess dreams are made of, really the most important thing is that my friends and family feel welcome. Everyone who comes to my home is greeted with a wagging tail.

CHAPTER 5

Remember her name

(FAME!)

Some (dogs) are born great, some achieve greatness, and some have greatness thrust upon them. All three apply in my case, obviously. I have no doubt that I was destined for a glamorous life from day one, but through charisma, uniqueness, nerve, and talent (OK, and a bit of good luck), I have found the limelight from time to time and ended up with a platform larger than I could have imagined when my dads and I first embarked on this journey.

I went from semi-recognizable Montrealer to internationally renowned iggy in a relatively short time. It can be dizzying for some to learn how to navigate newfound notoriety, but I was ready to embrace it thanks to a combination of good genes, a love of people, and my support network. Fame is a fickle puppy. On good days it can reward you with opportunities and treats galore, but on bad days you can feel as though the world is against you. Whether you're hoping for international stardom someday, or just want to be prepared should you suddenly find yourself a household name, I'm happy to share my strategies for handling life in the public eye.

Stay grounded

I never forget where I came from, and I stay close to the people who have supported me since the beginning of my journey. Any level of fame can be discombobulating, and if you're not careful it can change your sense of self and your core values. My support system keeps me grounded and reminds me of my roots, and I can trust that they love me for me and have my best interests at heart. Handling fame can be daunting unless you have the right people around you. Without support it can feel isolating, and it can be difficult to trust that the people vying for your attention aren't just after something.

I look back fondly on my early days, when a simple fleece sweater was a novelty for the folks passing by on my daily walks, and the photographic evidence was shared only with family and friends. In that sense I was lucky; I was used to being stopped on the street because of my outfits long before I found fame, so I was already adept at interacting with my public and making new friends on the go. I've been fortunate that my job has exposed me to a more diverse world of dogs and their companions, and led to important connections. As my fame and wardrobe have grown, so has my family, my circle of friends, my experiences around the world, and the love for my craft. These are the important things. Maintaining my core values and remaining humble ensure that I don't lose sight of what is most important, and that I continue to nurture the most integral relationships in my life.

Part of practicing humility means treating others with kindness, and offering a helping paw to those (brave souls) who look to me for guidance and advice. One rarely achieves success all on one's own. I'm grateful for the help I have received along the way and believe in continuing to pay that forward—I feel good about spreading my good furtune.

Work smarter, not harder

Although I'd love to be everywhere and everything all at once, I have learned to accept that it's just not possible. With heightened expectations of my productivity, a long list of responsibilities, and more people than ever vying for my attention, I've come to terms with the fact that there is no shame in delegating some tasks and lightening the load. I'm grateful to lean on my manager and my agent to handle the logistical elements of my life, so that I can focus on showing up and looking pretty. It's one thing to hustle, but there is no glamour in eschewing help from your support system and overworking yourself. Time is money, too, so there's no use in trying to do everything on your own. Trust your support network and let them help you. Teamwork makes the dreamwork.

Working smarter and not harder also means prioritizing tasks and obligations as urgent and/or important (my team helps with this, too, since I'm not much of a list-maker). If you don't take a beat, everything feels urgent. Everything is important! Everything must be done now! But this is very rarely true, and slowing down to make a plan with your team will ensure that you tackle your to-do list efficiently, and in a way that maximizes your time and enjoyment. My team also know how I like to wield my influence, and how to work around my nap schedule, so everyone wins.

If you're comfortable with it, fame can empower you. Once you learn the art of delegation, you can take comfort in knowing that your team has your back, and you can focus on nurturing your creative energy (and

napping). Leveraging my platform and influence for good is probably my favorite thing about being active on social media. I am so grateful that it allows me to promote important causes, and my colleagues allow me to make those connections and sort out all the details of potential collaborations.

Working with a team allows me to give the people what they want. No matter your profession—athlete, model, author, or, in my case, all three—without your audience you have nothing. Be sure to take the time to respond to positive messages and comments online when you can, and engage as much as possible with your audience. My team helps me go through suggestions from my fans: if they want merch, we start designing the line; if they want a coffee-table book ... we get on that (look at me go!). Keeping up with requests from my community also reinforces the importance of branching out. If you're a one-trick iggy, or if you're active on only one platform, you're limiting yourself. Old dogs absolutely *can* learn new tricks, so don't let anyone tell you otherwise.

Shake it off

It's a hard truth to accept, but the sooner you do so the easier your life will be: you will not be everyone's favorite dog treat. That doesn't mean there's anything wrong with you. There will always be people who want to see you fail, and you can't waste time worrying about what they think. To save my brain space for more important things, I like to live by the mantra "Stop caring what they think, and stop

You have places to be and treats to eat.

thinking they care." You have places to be and treats to eat, and you can't spend time dwelling on the people who don't want to be in your orbit.

At this point in the internet's history, it's well understood that being an online personality comes with a certain amount of vitriolic correspondence. It's sad, but true. Before getting defensive, I like to remind myself of the difference between kindly conveyed constructive criticism and personal attacks. If a friend is trying to tell me a slightly uncomfortable but necessary truth, I have to watch that I don't get fur on end and am humble enough to hear them out. But that's different from an ad hominem attack from a stranger on the internet. When dealing with unkind commentary online, my top piece of advice is to ignore, ignore, ignore. Don't feed the trolls!

If you *are* going to read the comments, make sure to be with friends and perhaps have some emotional-support cucumber snacks nearby. Keep in mind that human and dog brains alike could hear 100 nice things, but it will be the one negative comment that will be on repeat in your mind, so consume that negative content in moderation. In general, I don't advise engaging with negative commentary. It simply draws more attention to the offensive comment, and gives the commenter the attention they are seeking. However, sometimes I do decide to reply. I have three rules for my replies: it has to be sassy but not cruel, factual if you're hitting back at misinformation, and a one-time thing (I'm not getting into debates with commenters who aren't engaging in good faith).

If comments leave the land of kind-of-mean and stray into the territory of intentionally-cruel-and-harmful, recognize that for what it is: cyberbullying. There's no need to engage with cruelty, and harmful comments can be deleted and that user blocked. While I am a patient iggy and can appreciate a teachable moment, I have no time for hatred on my accounts. Remember that your online presence belongs to you, and no one is entitled to spread harmful messages on your platform.

If you find that monitoring any amount of online comments and messages is harming your mental health, set a boundary. You can alter the parameters on your social-media accounts to restrict or shut off comments and direct messages, or delegate the task of monitoring these aspects of your accounts to a member of your team. In any case, there is no reason to put your mental health at risk over unkind comments from strangers.

Another boundary I've set for myself relates to how much of my private life I share online. Keeping some aspects offline allows me to feel a bit more comfortable and in control. I'm happy for my online community to follow me to photo shoots and fashion shows, and even to the occasional mealtime or nap, but sometimes I like a quiet walk and some time to live my life without documenting every moment. Too much time online can also lead to comparisons between my life and the lives of other dogs, and comparison is the thief of joy. It's important to remember just how much of life happens offline.

Don't let the puparazzi get you down. Although I've rarely seen a picture of me that I didn't like, you can't count on the paps to have your best angles in mind, so don't let the occasional disappointing photo shake your confidence. Know your worth, and remember that you are more than a single photograph. These moments are also a great time to practice laughing at yourself. Sometimes I look ridiculous—it's part of my charm!

On and offline, stay humble, and stay true to who you are. Don't name-drop, don't chase clout, and don't waste time on people who aren't there for you. Don't change yourself for others, and don't dim your light. As my friend Lizzo says, if I'm shining, everybody's gonna shine.

Stick to self-care

There are expectations of you when you're a public personality. You may feel pulled in several directions at once, and it can be difficult to say no to requests for appearances, a quick pawtograph, or a meeting, but it's important to prioritize rest and self-care. You can't fill others' water bowls if yours is depleted, and I can't perform at my best if my batteries aren't recharged. If I need 20 hours of naps in a day (and I usually do), that is what I will do to make sure I feel my best and can continue to satisfy the standards I set for myself. After all, good isn't good enough when excellence is required.

Keeping a routine ensures that I practice my self-care strategies and activities regularly, and avoid burning out. I like to clear my head with a little exercise, and look forward to my long walk daily—unless it's too cold, too hot, too windy, or too rainy ... My dads ensure that I get a nice mix of my favorite treats and healthy meals every day,

and you already know how strongly I feel about staying hydrated. I like to plop down on one of my plush pillows to practice mindful breathing and meditation. If meditation turns into a nap, that's OK. I listen to my body, and when I'm pooched I take the rest I need.

As an ambitious iggy, I find it easy to get caught up in always striving for the next goal or milestone. My snoot is constantly sniffing out opportunities, but it is important to slow down regularly and take stock of the good in my life and the milestones I've reached with my team. To keep things in perspective, I like to start my day with a positive affirmation ("Mirror, mirror on the wall, who's the baddest bitch of all?") and keep a gratitude journal next to my bed. Even on a difficult day, I can always find three quick things to be grateful for (cucumber, Drew Barrymore, drag queens), and this helps me to keep things in perspective and be thankful for all the bright spots in my life.

TIKA'S
tunes

A good playlist has the power to get my tail wagging, even when I'm feeling down. Whether I'm primping for a magazine cover shoot, getting pumped to go to the dog park, or just having a kitchen dance party with my family, there's always a soundtrack to my day. Here are a few of my favorites:

- "J'irai où tu iras," Céline Dion

- "About Damn Time," Lizzo

- "I Feel Pretty," from *West Side Story* by Stephen Sondheim and Leonard Bernstein

- "I'm Alive," Céline Dion

- "Man! I Feel Like a Woman!," Shania Twain

- "It's the Time to Disco," from the film *Kal Ho Naa Ho* (2003)

- "Your Disco Needs You," Kylie Minogue

- "Believe," Cher

- "Lay All Your Love on Me," ABBA

- "It's All Coming Back to Me Now," Céline Dion

ADVEN-
TURES

in your own
backyard

Adventure is a state of mind, not a specific place. Whether you're getting to know a new city, looking to make the most of a staycation, or just keen to shake up your daily routine, don't overlook the potential of what lies right at your paws.

While I love to globe-trot and travel to far-off places, there are plenty of good reasons to have fun close to home. It's better for the environment, better for your wallet (or so my dads tell me), requires less logistical wrangling and planning, and allows you to appreciate what is right in front of you.

I've lived my whole life in beautiful Tiohtià:ke, which is on the traditional territory of the Kanien'keha:ka Nation, also known as the city of Montreal, Quebec. There is so much to see and do in the city that I don't think I could ever be bored—and besides, the streets smell slightly different every day! If you're feeling you need a change of scene and pace, look no further than where you are. And just in case you plan on visiting my hometown, I'll let you know about some of my favorite spots.

Play tourist

We're usually given tips on how *not* to look like a tourist (hide your map, stop taking cliché selfies, stay off the beaten path), but it can be a lot of fun to channel your inner tourist around your own stomping grounds. Pretend you're about to host a friend who has never been to your neck of the woods. Where would you take them? Make an itinerary with all the hits, and treat yourself to touristy outings. Often we overlook attractions that we live next to, and it can be fun to see your home through the fresh eyes of a tourist. Get to the zoo to see the penguins, admire the art at a gallery, stop to smell the roses at the botanic garden, or just post up at a trendy bistro to people-watch. The cheesier the activity, the better. Find the best spot to watch the sunset, buy a postcard to send to a friend you've been meaning to get in touch with, lose yourself in unfamiliar streets. Just be sure to take lots of pictures.

Staycation formula

You can expand your world without even expanding your regular radius. I realize that you may be reading this from a location in the world that isn't mine, but I've found that there's a standard equation for a fabulous staycation. Sustenance + activities + fresh air = a great outing. A more detailed example for you: the day starts with a walk to a local cafe, where I get a fresh treat and my company gets a coffee to go for a stroll at the local dog park or along some other scenic route. Next, we take in some culture, whether that be entertainment from buskers or admiring some amazing murals. I'll need another snack and hydration stop after that, so then it's time for a picnic lunch and maybe another local outdoor attraction, before settling into a chic terrace that welcomes canine customers for a wind-down with something nice to sip (cucumber water for me, please). This staycation math is transferable

Sustenance + activities + fresh air

---

a great outing

to any location, really, so apply it whether you're close to home or far, far away.

A staycation can be as varied as the people embarking upon it. Just like any trip, it can be planned on a shoestring or as a splurge. If I'm keeping my staycation on a budget, I like to scour local events for free entertainment, dog meet-ups (some of the cutest gatherings you'll ever see, if I do say so myself), outdoor festivals, or movies in the park. Pack up some picnic snacks, a cozy blanket, and maybe a squeaky toy or two and I can bask in a sunny park for hours. Have lunch next to a river or canal, or rent a boat to see the city from the water. I truly love frolicking in city greenspaces (my faves in Montreal are Parc La Fontaine and Jarry Park—just don't give the squirrels any treats; save those for me!).

If I'm looking to really treat myself, my staycation will take me for a night or two to one of my favorite hotels for some luxurious pampering. There's something especially rejuvenating about a plush hotel bathrobe, room service, and a different bedtime view. Treat yourself to a night out on the town knowing that your bed for the night is already made at a five-star hotel, then come back to whatever cheesy movie is on TV (fingers crossed it's *Legally Blonde*), and head off to dreamland on as many pillows as possible. Make sure you don't have a wake-up call set, and put the do-not-disturb sign on the door handle—it's time for a swanky snooze.

Seasons change

Taking advantage of urban oases doesn't cost a thing, and it's one of my favorite ways to enjoy the city in all seasons. In the spring, we stop to smell the flowers, in the summer I bask while my dads tan. The autumn foliage provides the most beautiful backdrops for my fall outfit photo shoots, and although I'd probably be happy hibernating through the winter, even I have to admit that everything looks beautiful under a blanket of snow. (And although I'd recommend it as winter fun for everyone else, don't you dare try to put me on a toboggan!)

A familiar place can feel totally different from season to season, and I embrace them all, even winter. Northern hemisphere cities can be home to lots of winter fun, and Montreal is no exception. There's Igloofest, the coldest music festival I know of, outdoor ice slides and skating (again, something I only want to observe, but still fun events to dress for), and frosty light shows. After I've put in my outdoor time, there's nothing better than defrosting in a cafe and watching others brave the elements in the name of amusement. I always have a great nap after glacial outings. Once the warm weather returns, it's almost impossible to keep up with the many festivals and events. If you blink you might miss an outdoor DJ or concert you were looking forward to, so I recommend putting some handy reminders in your calendar for maximum fun-in-the-sun scheduling.

List it

Speaking of calendar reminders, putting in a little time to look at logistics will help you keep track of all the potential fun you can look forward to. It can be a seasonal list (hot iggy summer … and fall, winter, and spring), a thematic list (all the best parks, all the best views, all the best hikes, all the best street food, all the best free museum days, and so on), or a more traditional bucket list of only the top experiences you want to chase around town.

Building a staycation bucket list can help you decide what kind of trip you're keen on, and it means you'll always have a quick way to decide on something to do. Make sure your list doesn't induce any stress or FOMO, though. Frame it as a wish list rather than a to-do list, so that there's no real urgency to cross things off it, and if you miss something it just means you have more to look forward to. I do also love the sense of accomplishment that comes with crossing something off a list.

A spot with a view

There's nothing like a different vantage point to see your city anew. Most cities have them, and in Montreal it's La Grande Roue in the Old Port, a Ferris wheel that offers a bird's-eye view of the city all year round. There are also the lookouts from the Oratoire de St-Joseph, and Parc du Mont-Royal, and indoors at the Montreal Tower. A viewpoint isn't the only way to get a new perspective on

a place, though; you can hop on a bus tour, rent a bike, go for a paddle, or even explore the metro, if there is one.

Hometown history

How well do you know wherever you call home? I'm always learning more about the history of my hometown. In Canada, that has meant learning about the legacy and lasting impact of colonialism. A good place for my dads to start was at native-land.ca to learn about the Indigenous territory we live and play within.

There are plenty of resources online to learn about the history of any given place, and you can often find organized walking tours or information for self-guided walks to learn while you stroll. If you're feeling ambitious or in the mood for games, you can even create a kind of scavenger hunt to help you explore your city. Challenge yourself to learn about public art installations, historical buildings, and even what trees are most prevalent in your part of the world. You never know what fun facts or important history you'll stumble on.

The Village

Formerly known as Montreal's Gay Village, "The Village" as it's known now is an internationally recognized LGBTQIA2+ destination, enjoyed by over a million visitors every year. In the summer it's pedestrianized, which is perfect for popping into the local stores and restaurants, enjoying art installations, and simply showing off my colorful outfits around the time of Pride every year. The Village has been thriving and evolving for decades, and continues to strive to be a welcoming and inclusive place for all. As a gay icon you better believe that I love to prance through it. It's always a bonus if it's a sunny day and I get to sit on a patio to enjoy a drag show—I promise not to try to steal the spotlight.

Neighborhood noshing

A great way to explore a city is to go neighborhood by neighborhood. In Montreal I love strutting through the ornate gates to explore Chinatown, which has the honor of being designated the city's first historic site as well as being home to incredible Asian cuisine. I head to the artsy Mile End neighborhood for my favorite bagels at St-Viateur, find the hip cafes and eateries in Le Plateau, and zip over to St-Zotique so my dads can enjoy espresso, cannolis, and pizza in Little Italy (that's *amore*!). We love grabbing a drink and a seat in the Quartier des Spectacles to enjoy whatever festival has taken over the area, or wandering the cobblestone streets of the Old Port to admire the architecture and the ambiance.

Many cities have markets that are an attraction in their own right. The vibrant open-air ones are the perfect place to stock up on picnic fixings, sample the bounty from local farms and specialty producers, or simply stop for a bite to eat. I've lived a short walk from both the Jean-Talon and Atwater markets in Montreal, and I love starting my day

with a stroll among the colorful stalls. If you're lucky, you may get offers of samples as you make your way through, although of course that may just be because of my sweet snoot. While my dads pick up ingredients from the market, I like to take the opportunity to strut my stuff and meet the friendly folks in my neighborhood. You know how the saying goes: to market, to market, to show off your outfit!

Bloom where you're planted

Of course, if you want me or any fellow furry friends to join you on these adventures, my number one tip would be to look up dog-friendly places before you set out. Outdoor activities are always a safe bet, as are many restaurants and cafes with outdoor seating.

Exploring your surroundings allows you to create connections with your community and all the people who make it special. While I love finding novel experiences nearby, I really appreciate being a regular at my local cafe, where the baristas know my little brother and me and always have time to stop and chat. I love saying hello to familiar faces at the park, or visiting the same farmer at the market who always has the freshest cucumbers. Creating adventures close to home doesn't require much, just a spunky attitude. A place that seems old hat can feel totally different depending on the time of day, the season, your adventure buddies, and even your state of mind. Home is where the heart is, and I know stopping to appreciate my home always warms my heart.

Author Acknowledgements

Thomas and Katherine Shapiro are twins who are thrilled to collaborate on this project with Tika the Iggy. For more Tika, find her @tikatheiggy on Instagram, TikTok, and YouTube.

Thomas is very proud to be Tika's "second-favourite dad." He is also a photographer, costume designer, and content creator just to name a few. Thomas would like to thank his and Tika's extended family, friends both online and off, and Tika's community for their incredible support over the years. A special thank you to his husband Louis, and children Harrison and Eleanor for their love and support.

Katherine is a freelance writer from Ottawa. She would like to thank Tika and Thomas for bringing her along for this ride, and her family and friends for putting up with too many dog puns. It's always a joy to step into Tika's world.